Perfect Panama

Recipes

A Go-To Cookbook of Latin American Dish
Ideas!

BY

Julia Chiles

OOOOOOOOOOOOOOOOOOOOOOOOOOOOOOOOOOOOO

License Notes

OOOOOOOOOOOOOOOOOOOOOOOOOOOOOOOOOOOOOOOO

Table of Contents

Introduction

Panamanian recipes sound exotic and interesting, don't they?

Wouldn't you like to make real Panama dishes right in your own kitchen?

Can you find suitable ingredients to create authentic meals at home?

Yes! You can find all kinds of the same or similar foods to let you create meals just like those prepared and enjoyed in Panama. Most of the fruits indigenous to Panama can be found in many other areas, including bananas, papayas, oranges, watermelons, passion fruit, pineapples and more.

The vegetables you'll need to make authentic recipes include yams, yuca, potatoes, beets, squash and corn.

The corn-based recipes from Panama start with kernels of corn that are cooked and ground to make dough. (This is different than in other countries that start with corn flour.) Panamanians use fresh corn in lunch and dinner recipes, too.

Since Panama is a multi-cultural country, between two land masses, its dishes have been influenced by Caribbean and Latin American countries. Read on, let's cook Panamanian...

Panamanian breakfasts are unique and tasty. Here are a few favorites...

Corn Dough in Banana Leaves – Bollos

This is a wonderful corn recipe served in Panama. It's very simple, and celebrates the sweet, gorgeous taste of fresh corn, husk-on.

Makes 18-20 bollos

Cooking + Prep Time: 1 hour 20 minutes

Ingredients:

- 6 husk-on ears of corn, fresh
- 2 heaping tbsp. of polenta
- 1 pinch sugar, granulated
- 1/4 tsp. of salt, kosher

Instructions:

De-husk corn ears. Discard silks. Place husks in bowl with hot water and allow them to soften.

Cut kernels from corn cobs. Puree in your food processor. Then strain them through sieve, getting most liquid from pureed corn.

Place corn puree, sugar, polenta kosher salt in medium bowl. Combine well. Remove husks from bowl of water. Fill them with 2 tbsp. corn each. Roll husks up. Tie ends with twine, then place them in steamer. Continue till all corn puree is used up.

Cover and steam the bollos for 35 to 40 minutes. Serve while hot.

Breakfast Meat in Tomato Sauce

It is a popular breakfast dish, and it is sometimes served at other meals, too. It goes so well when you serve it over white steamed rice.

Makes 4 Servings

Cooking + Prep Time: 2 hours 20 minutes

Ingredients:

- 1 x 8-oz. can of tomato sauce, low sodium
- 1/4 cup of sauce, sofrito
- 1 small packet of sazon seasoning blend
- 1/2 tsp. of oregano, dried
- 1 tbsp. of adobo seasoning
- Salt, kosher, as desired
- 2 lbs. of stew meat, beef
- 2 cups of potatoes, peeled and cubed
- 1 cup of water, filtered

Instructions:

Combine sofrito sauce, tomato sauce, adobo seasoning, sazon seasoning blend, salt and oregano in large sized pot. Simmer on med-low for five minutes.

Add the stew meat. Cook till browned evenly. Add and stir in enough water to barely cover the meat. Cover pot. Simmer for an hour or so.

Add the potatoes. Cook for 25 minutes to 1/2 hour, till potatoes have become tender. Serve.

Fried Plantains

It is a traditional side dish for breakfast or lunch in Panama. It's simple to make, just by frying slices of ripe plantains in oil.

Makes 4-6 Servings

Cooking + Prep Time: 50 minutes

Ingredients:

- 4 green plantains, unripe, large
- 4 cups of water, warm
- Salt, kosher, as desired
- 2 cups of oil, vegetable

To serve: ketchup

Instructions:

Pour four cups water and 1 tbsp. kosher salt in large sized bowl. Set it aside.

Cut ends from plantains. Cut lengthways and slit through the peel. Beginning at the slit, pry the peel off.

Cut the plantains crossways in pieces of 1" thickness. Place in medium bowl with lightly salted, warm water. Allow to sit for 18-20 minutes.

Heat 1/2" of oil in heavy skillet on med. heat till oil sizzles when you add a small piece of plantain. Remove the pieces of plantain from water. Fully blot dry.

Place plantains in oil, without crowding them. Turn occasionally while frying till they are tender and just starting to turn a golden color, about five to seven minutes.

Remove plantains with tongs to work surface. Spray glass tumbler bottom with non-stick spray. Flatten plantains gently till they are 1/4-inch thick. Slide glass from plantains.

Return flat plantains to the oil, on med. heat. Turn occasionally wile frying till golden brown, three to four minutes.

Transfer plantain pieces to plate lined with paper towels. Don't blot them. Sprinkle using salt. Serve promptly, with ketchup, if desired.

Panama has a wide variety of recipes for lunch, dinner, appetizers and side dishes. Here are some of the best...

Chicken Plantain Stew

This recipe works well for dinner for large families, or family and friends. It's a Latin American style chicken stew with plantains and cassava root. There are many varieties on this dish, but this is a special one.

Makes 12 Servings

Cooking + Prep Time: 2 hours

Ingredients:

- 9 cups of water, filtered
- 1 chicken, whole
- 2 peeled, 2"-cut plantains
- 1 chopped onion, medium
- 1/2 cup of chopped cilantro, fresh
- 5 chopped garlic cloves
- 1 1/2 tsp. of salt, sea
- 3 lbs. of peeled, 1"-cubed cassava (yuca) roots
- 6 quartered small potatoes, white
- 1 x 15 1/4-oz. can of drained corn

Instructions:

Combine the water with chicken, onions, plantains, garlic, cilantro and sea salt in large sized pot. Bring to boil. Lower heat level to med. Cook till the chicken isn't pink at bone anymore. Juices should be running clear, which takes 45 minutes or so. Meat thermometer should read 165F.

Remove chicken. Allow it to cool. Add corn, yuca and potatoes to soup. Cook on med. heat till potatoes and yuca have softened, 1/2 hour or so.

Discard chicken bones and skin. Place the meat back in soup and combine by stirring. Serve hot.

Chicheme Sweet Drink

This drink is simple and refreshing, and sweetly complex. There is some flexibility in the recipe, meaning that you can add pinches of your favorite spices to tailor it to your taste.

Makes 3 cups

Cooking + Prep Time: 20 minutes + 15 minutes refrigeration time

Ingredients:

- 1/4 pound corn, fresh
- Sugar, granulated, as desired
- 4 sticks of cinnamon
- 2 tsp. of nutmeg, ground
- 3 cups milk, evaporated
- 1 tbsp. corn starch
- Vanilla, as desired

Instructions:

Wash the corn. Boil with sticks of cinnamon. Once corn is soft, remove from heat. Add vanilla, nutmeg, diluted corn starch and sugar. Stir and combine well and place in refrigerator till cold. Serve on ice.

Panamanian Gingerbread

It is one of the easier recipes for Panamanian gingerbread. It's the type that is often sold in Panama's Chiriqui province, and it includes fresh ginger, giving it a delicious taste, especially with milk.

Makes 70 slices

Cooking + Prep Time: 50 minutes + 2-3 hours cooling time

Ingredients:

- 7 1/4 cups of flour, all-purpose
- 1/2 tsp. of salt, kosher
- 1/2 tsp. of low sodium baking powder
- 1/2 cup of shortening, vegetable
- 3/4 lb. of minced ginger root, fresh
- 2 pints of molasses, pure

Instructions:

Preheat oven to 450F. Grease, then flour 15" x 20" baking dish. Then whisk flour, baking powder and salt together in medium bowl.

Mix ginger, molasses and shortening together till you have a smooth texture. Add and stir in flour mixture till there are no remaining dry lumps. Pour mixture into baking dish.

Bake in 450F oven till toothpick pressed into middle comes back clean, usually 40-45 minutes or so. Allow to cook for 12-15 minutes and slice in 2" squares. Allow to cool for two to three hours longer and serve.

Carne Guisada

This dish is made with potatoes braised with tomatoes and tender slices of beef, for an easy dinner any night of the week. It's tasty and hearty, especially when served over rice.

Makes 4 Servings

Cooking + Prep Time: 1 hour 25 minutes

Ingredients:

- 1 tbsp. of oil, olive
- 1 peeled, chopped onion, medium
- 2 garlic cloves
- 2 lbs. of thin-sliced chuck steak
- 3 chopped Roma tomatoes, large
- 1 seeded, minced jalapeno pepper
- 1 cup of beef broth or water
- 2 peeled, cubed potatoes, medium
- Kosher salt ground pepper, as desired

Instructions:

Heat the oil in wide skillet on med. heat.

Add garlic and onions. Cook till they soften.

Add beef. Cook till browned lightly.

Add the tomatoes. Mash with back of spoon while cooking till they soften and release their juices.

Add broth or water. Bring to boil and skim away any scum that eventually floats to top. Add the chili peppers.

Lower the heat level and cover. Simmer for 40-50 minutes, till beef becomes tender.

Add the potatoes. Cook for 8-10 minutes, till tender. Sauce should be thickened and reduced.

Season as desired and serve while hot.

Panamanian Pepper Steak

This is a favorite recipe for many, because it uses some ingredients that you usually will have in the pantry or fridge. It's also an easy dish to make, and adjustable for your personal tastes.

Makes 4 Servings

Cooking + Prep Time: 55 minutes

Ingredients:

- 2 tbsp. of oil, olive
- 1 chopped onion, medium
- 2 thin-sliced bell peppers, large
- 2 minced garlic cloves
- 1/3 cup of low sodium soy sauce
- 1/3 cup of honey, pure
- 1/3 cup of vinegar, red wine
- 1 1/2 lbs. of thin-strip-cut flank steak

Instructions:

Heat the oil in skillet on med. heat. Cook bell peppers, garlic and onions in the oil till they are tender but crisp, while frequently stirring. Set them aside.

Heat large sized skillet on med-high. Pour vinegar, soy sauce and honey into skillet. Add the beef. Stir the beef frequently while cooking till done evenly, 10-15 minutes. Add and stir in the cooked veggies. Cook for 10-15 minutes more and serve.

Corn Cakes

These subtly crispy tortillas are a lovely golden in color and delicious to eat. They make an excellent side dish with so many main dishes.

Makes 5 Servings

Cooking + Prep Time: 1/2 hour

Ingredients:

- 1 cup of water, filtered
- 1 cup of corn tortilla mix, instant
- 1/4 tsp. of salt, kosher
- 1 tbsp. of flour, rice

Optional:

- 1 pinch of sugar, granulated
- 1 tbsp. of butter, unsalted

Instructions:

Mix water, tortilla mix, rice flour, sugar (if using) and salt in med. bowl.

Wet your hands and knead mixture, forming "masa".

Form masa bunches in circles. Be sure to pinch the edges. Thickness should be consistent at 1/3 or 3/4 inches thick.

Place some butter in pan, evenly spreading it. Heat over med-high. When hot, place circles of masa on pan. Allow them to bake, flipping every couple of minutes so they won't burn. They should become golden and start puffing up. Be careful not to overcook.

Repeat steps till you have baked all circles. Serve.

Panamanian Chicken Noodle Soup

This is a very hearty soup, just perfect for those cold days, or days when you're feeling under the weather. It's so rich in taste and easy to make, too.

Makes 6 Servings

Cooking + Prep Time: 2 hours 5 minutes

Ingredients:

- 6 skinned chicken legs
- 1 chopped onion, large
- 1 chopped bell pepper, green
- 1 de-seeded, minced chili pepper, hot
- 1/3 chopped bell pepper, red
- 4 minced garlic cloves
- 3 cups of stock, chicken
- 2 ears of cut corn, fresh
- 2 sliced celery stalks
- 2 sliced carrots
- 2 tbsp. chili pepper puree
- 2 tbsp. of sofrito sauce, prepared
- 4 minced cilantro leaves
- 1/2 cup of pasta, orzo
- 1 tsp. leaves of oregano

Instructions:

Place the chicken legs in large sized pan on med. heat. Add green bell peppers, onions, red bell peppers, hot chili peppers and the garlic. Cover the pot. Cook till vegetables have softened, 30-35 minutes or so.

Pour the stock in pan. Bring to boil. Simmer till chicken isn't pink at bone anymore. Juice should run clear, 45 minutes or longer.

Add celery, corn, carrots, chili pepper puree, cilantro and sofrito sauce. Cook the soup till these vegetables soften, 30 minutes or longer.

Add and stir in oregano and orzo. Cook till pasta has become tender, 12-15 minutes or so, and serve.

Bistec Picado

This spicy, enticing stir fry melds garlic, green peppers and onions together in a beautiful way. The seasonings help to transform even tough beef cuts into bites of mouthwatering goodness.

Makes 4 Servings

Cooking + Prep Time: 1 hour 15 minutes

Ingredients:

- 1 1/2 pounds of beef tenderloin
- 2 tbsp. of oil, vegetable
- 4 or 5 wedge-cut Roma tomatoes, fresh
- 2 cups of water, filtered, as needed
- 1 large, thin-sliced onion, white
- 3 chopped cloves of garlic
- 1 x 1" chunk-cut bell pepper, any color
- 2 thin-sliced jalapeño peppers
- 1 tsp. of cumin, ground
- 1 tsp. of cilantro, dried
- 1 tsp. of pepper, ground
- 2 tbsp. of chili powder
- Salt, kosher, as desired

Instructions:

Heat large fry pan on med-high. Brown beef. Drain it on plate lined with paper towels.

Add oil to pan. Heat for a minute or so. Add onions. Cook till translucent.

Add jalapeno, bell peppers, tomatoes and garlic. Add beef back in.

Add and stir in the seasonings.

Slowly add water to JUST cover vegetable and beef mixture. You might not need two cups. Bring water to boil.

Cover pan with lid and lower heat level to med. Cook and stir frequently for 35-40 minutes or so. Don't allow liquid to evaporate fully.

Serve with warm tortillas, beans or rice.

Whitefish Ceviche

Panama is a land blessed with many sources of fresh fish. Most areas have arrivals daily fresh fish, and this ceviche is just one example of how they make wonderful dishes.

Makes 6-8 Servings

Cooking + Prep Time: 35 minutes + 24 hours refrigeration time + 1 hour soaking time

Ingredients:

- 3 to 5 pounds of fish fillet, boneless, white
- 3 onions, white
- 1 pepper, red
- 1 pepper, green
- 2 celery stalks
- 2 cups of lime juice, fresh
- Aji chombo Panamanian pepper
- Cilantro

Instructions:

Cut the fish in 1/4-inch cubes.

Soak the cubes of fish in salted water for about an hour and drain them well.

Dice the celery, peppers, onions, cilantro, aji chombo and garlic. Add to large-sized bowl.

Add the fish and salt. Pour lime juice over the top. Cover. Refrigerate for a day.

Serve on lettuce or with patacones or crackers.

Panamanian Potato Salad

Potato salad in Panama is a lovely pink color, since a beet is often tossed in. The color shouldn't discourage you – this is a tasty, popular food at Panamanian parties.

Makes 4 Servings

Cooking + Prep Time: 1 1/4 hour

Ingredients:

- 4 potatoes, medium
- 1 finely diced carrot
- 1 diced celery stalk
- 1 onion, medium
- 1 cup of chopped parsley, fresh
- 1 garlic clove
- 1 beet
- 1 egg, large
- 1/2 cup of mayonnaise, reduced fat
- 1 tsp. of mustard
- Kosher salt ground pepper, as desired

Instructions:

Boil potatoes in large sized pot. When half-cooked, add carrot and beet. Add egg for final 10 minutes of potatoes cooking.

Dice and chop garlic, onion, celery and parsley.

Drain pot of potatoes. They should be tender, as should carrot and beet. Egg should by now be hard-boiled.

Peel and dice the carrot and beet and chop up egg.

Mix mustard, mayo, garlic, onion, celery, egg and parsley into deep bowl.

Add remainder of ingredients. Mix only enough to coat vegetables with mayo mixture. Season as desired and serve fully.

Panamanian Seafood Stew

You'll probably be amazed at how quickly and easily this seafood dish comes together. The sofrito can be made the day before, so it's a great dish for entertaining.

Makes 6-8 Servings

Cooking + Prep Time: 55 minutes

Ingredients:

For sofrito

- 4 tbsp. of oil, olive
- 2 thin-strip-sliced onions, white
- 1 1/2 thin-strip sliced peppers, green
- 1 1/2 thin-strip sliced peppers, red
- 1/2 cup of thin-sliced onions, green
- 1 cup of chopped cilantro, fresh
- 3 minced cloves of garlic
- 2 envelopes of Sazón seasoning
- 2 tbsp. of tomato paste, low sodium
- 1 bay leaf, small

For rice

- 6 cups of water, filtered
- 2 cups of rice, long-grain
- To finish
- 4 cups of stock, seafood
- 1 tsp. of oregano
- Sea salt ground pepper, as desired
- 1 x 24-ounce bag seafood mix (crab meat, octopus, mussels, shrimp, calamari)

Instructions:

Heat oil in heavy, large skillet on med-high. Add onions, peppers, garlic, bay leaf and cilantro. Cook for four to five minutes, till they begin softening. Add tomato paste and sazon seasoning blend. Cook for three more minutes. Set mixture aside.

Add six cups filtered water to large-sized pot. Bring to boil. Add two cups rice. Cook for 8-10 minutes and stir often. Set rice aside.

Remove a cup of the sofrito. Reserve for later.

Heat skillet with sofrito on med. heat. Add rice and remainder of water with rice, four cups stock, sea salt, ground pepper and oregano. Cook for five minutes more.

Add seafood mixture. Stir constantly while cooking for five minutes more. Top with reserved sofrito and serve promptly.

Puff Pastry with Meat Peppers

It is one of the easiest puff pastry dishes to prepare. Plus, you can make it with minced pork, beef or chicken, so it's quite versatile.

Makes 6 Servings

Cooking + Prep Time: 45 minutes

Ingredients:

- 5 small pieces from one garlic clove (they are sometimes called "teeth")
- 3 medium peppers, green
- 1 leek
- Oil, olive
- Sea salt ground pepper
- 1 lb. of chicken, minced
- 1 egg, large
- 2 sheets puff pastry, holjadre

Instructions:

Add a bit of oil to medium pan. Chop peppers, leek and garlic and add. Allow to cook for a couple minutes.

Add chicken meat. Stir for several minutes. Remove when done.

Spread puff pastry in baking dish. Prick using a fork. Pour already cooked ingredients in and close top of pastry.

Paint top with egg. Place in 350F oven for 20 minutes or so. Serve hot.

Slow Cooker Beef Spices

This delectable dish features tender shreds of beef stewed with tomatoes, peppers, and tasty spices. It is often served with plantains, rice or black beans.

Makes 6-7 Servings

Cooking + Prep Time: 25 minutes + 6 hours slow cooker time

Ingredients:

- 1 tbsp. of oil, canola
- 2 lbs. chuck roast, boneless
- Salt, kosher
- Pepper, ground
- 1 peeled, sliced lengthwise into halves carrot
- 1 seeded, thinly sliced bell pepper, green
- 1 seeded, thinly sliced bell pepper, red
- 1 peeled, then halved thinly sliced medium onion, yellow
- 10 peeled, chopped garlic cloves
- 1/2 cup of white wine, dry
- 2 cups of tomato puree, canned
- 1 x 6-oz. can of tomato paste, low sodium
- 1 cup of chicken broth, low salt
- 1 tsp. of cumin, ground
- 1 tsp. of oregano, dried
- 1 bay leaf, medium
- 1/2 cup of green olives, sliced
- 1 tbsp. of vinegar, white

For garnishing

- 1/2 cup of chopped cilantro leaves, fresh

- 1-2 limes, wedge-cut

Instructions:

Season the meat on either side using 1 tsp. of kosher salt a few grinds of pepper. Heat the oil in heavy skillet. Brown meat on high for three minutes each side. Transfer to slow cooker. Add carrot slices.

Add 1 tbsp. oil to skillet. Add peppers, garlic and onions. Reduce heat level to med. Cook for six to seven minutes and constantly stir for first minute, till vegetables soften and begin caramelizing.

Add the wine. Simmer for one minute or so, while stirring and scraping any browned bits from pan. Transfer mixture to slow cooker.

Whisk tomato paste, tomato puree, 2 tsp. of salt and the dried spices in medium-sized bowl. Pour on top of meat in slow cooker. Cook using high setting for six hours. Remove meat after five and a half hours. Use two forks to shred and return it to slow cooker.

Add and stir in the vinegar and olives. Cook for another half-hour. Garnish with lime wedges and chopped cilantro. Serve with black beans or white rice.

Garlic Pork Roast

It is a rather lengthy recipe, but it results in a fall-apart meat dish with tons of flavor. It is often served with pinto beans in ham stock.

Makes 8 Servings

Cooking + Prep Time: 5 hours 40 minutes + 1 hour marinating time

Ingredients:

- 3 to 5 lb. pork shoulder, boneless
- 1 tbsp. of oil, vegetable
- 1 bunch of minced cilantro
- 1 wedge-cut lime, fresh

For marinating

- 1/2 cup of lime juice, fresh
- 1/2 cup of orange juice, fresh
- 15 minced garlic cloves
- 1 tbsp. of cumin, ground
- 2 tbsp. of salt, kosher
- 1 tbsp. of pepper, ground
- 1/2 cup of chopped cilantro
- 4 tbsp. of oil, olive
- Additional kosher salt ground pepper

Instructions:

Combine marinating ingredients in large-sized zipper top plastic bag. Debone and deskin the pork shoulder, if necessary. Add to marinade. Coat well. Marinate for an hour or longer in your refrigerator. Overnight is even better.

Remove roast from bag. Truss using string to keep it together. Salt meat side of roast once again.

Preheat oven to 400 degrees F. Then heat 1 tbsp. oil on med-high in large-sized Dutch oven. Sear pork with skin side facing up. Add salt ground pepper to fat side of pork. Transfer roast from Dutch oven to oven. Cook at 400 degrees F for one hour. After that hour, lower oven temperature to 300 degrees F. Cook for four more hours. Roast temp should be about 195F.

Remove roast from oven. Cover with lid. Allow it resting for a little while and serve.

Panamanian Fried Snapper

It is an easy recipe to make; moreover, the flavor is simple but delicious. The pickled vegetables and peppers complement the snapper so well.

Makes 2 Servings

Cooking + Prep Time: 30 minutes

Ingredients:

- 1 x 1 1/2-lb. cleaned, scaled whole snapper, red
- Sea salt ground pepper, as desired
- To fry: 1 quart of oil, vegetable
- 1 tsp. of oil, vegetable
- 1/2 sliced onion, white
- 1/8 tsp. of garlic, minced
- 1/2 peeled, thin-sliced carrot, large
- 1 sprig of leaf-stripped thyme, fresh
- 1 cracked berry, allspice
- 1/4 seeded, minced pepper, habanero
- 1/4 cup of vinegar, white
- 1 tbsp. of water, filtered
- 3/4 tsp. of salt, kosher
- 1 pinch of sugar, brown

Instructions:

Pat fish dry. Slice three slits in each side. Season all sides using sea salt kosher pepper.

Heat 1 qt. of oil in large-sized skillet on med-high till it smokes. Place fish carefully in this pan. Fry till crisp and browned, five minutes per side or so. Remove the fish. Place on plate lined with paper towels.

Heat a tsp. of oil in large-sized skillet on med-high. Stir carrot, onion and garlic into pan. Stir while cooking for one to two minutes. Add allspice, thyme, vinegar, habanero pepper, filtered water, sugar and kosher salt. Continue to cook till onions soften and liquid reduces, five minutes or so.

Garnish fish with onion mixture on top and serve.

Coconut Chicken Pasta

This chicken and pasta with coconut milk has a warm and gorgeous flavor. The sauce is silky, with plenty of veggies, to make a simple and complete meal.

Makes 2 Servings

Cooking + Prep Time: 1 hour 5 minutes + 1/2 hour marinating time

Ingredients:

- 1 pound of breast, chicken
- 3 or 4 garlic cloves
- 2 tsp. of jerk seasoning
- 1/2 small yellow or green pepper, sweet
- 1 tomato, small
- 1 pkg. of pasta, penne
- 1 tbsp. of butter, unsalted
- 1/2 tsp. of salt, kosher
- Optional: 1/4 cup of cheese shreds
- 3/4 cup of milk, coconut

Instructions:

Chop the chicken in bite-sized pieces. Season using 1 tsp. of jerk seasoning. Allow to marinate for about a half-hour. Grill or bake breasts for 20 minutes or so.

Cook the pasta using package directions. Drain it and set it aside.

Heat the butter. Sauté green pepper, garlic and tomato for three to five minutes.

Add the coconut milk, kosher salt extra jerk seasoning, if using. Cook for three to five minutes over med. heat while stirring.

Fold pasta into mixture. Combine well. Add the chicken.

Sprinkle cheese shreds on top, if using. Serve promptly.

Pork Ceviche

This pork belly dish is served in many homes and some local restaurants in Panama. It started as a lower class type of meal, since it uses pork belly, but it has the unique taste that many people love.

Makes 4 Servings

Cooking + Prep Time: 45 minutes + 1 hour refrigerator marinating time

Ingredients:

- 1 pound of cubed pork belly
- 1/2 cup of vinegar, white
- 1 diced cucumber, small
- 1 tsp. of sugar, brown
- 1 sliced small onion, yellow
- 1 piece of Thai chili, small
- Salt, kosher pepper, ground, as desired
- 1 tsp. of oil, vegetable
- 1 lime, small

Instructions:

Heat oil in med-sized pan. Spread cubed pork evenly in pan and brown it. Remove pan from heat. Set it aside.

Combine sugar, chilies and vinegar in small-sized bowl. Season as desired and combine well.

Place cucumber and seared pork cubes in large-sized bowl. Add the onions. Combine thoroughly. Pour vinegar mixture into the bowl. Toss well. Then squeeze a lime on top of mixture.

Place pork ceviche in refrigerator and allow to marinate in juices for an hour or so. Serve.

Peas with Rice

If you're looking for a dish for holiday meals, this could be it. Rice and peas make a wonderful combination, and they are served as essentials on holiday menus.

Makes 4 Servings

Cooking + Prep Time: 50 minutes

Ingredients:

- 8 3/4 oz. of bacon bits, real
- 2 cups of rice, uncooked
- 1 can of garden peas, fresh
- 1 roughly chopped onion, medium

Instructions:

Fry chopped onions till glazed as you desire.

Add bacon bits. Cook till done.

Add rice to pot, along with 4 cups filtered water. Season as desired.

Bring to boil, then cover pot. Lower temperature to cook rice. Combine and serve.

Carimañolas

It is an ideally side dish or appetizer for your whole family to enjoy. You can substitute ground turkey for the ground beef if you like.

Makes 10 Servings

Cooking + Prep Time: 1/2 hour

Ingredients:

- 1 1/2 lbs. of peeled, chunk-cut fresh or frozen yuca
- Salt, kosher, as desired
- To fry: oil, vegetable

For the filling

- 2 tbsp. of oil, vegetable
- 1 minced garlic clove
- 1/4 cup of chopped bell pepper, red
- 1/4 cup of onion, chopped
- 1 chopped scallion, small
- Salt, kosher, as desired
- Pepper, ground, as desired
- 1/2 tsp. of cumin, ground
- 1 tbsp. of tomato paste, low sodium
- 1/2 pound of beef, ground

Instructions:

Place yuca, water enough to cover it and kosher salt in large-sized pot. Bring to boil. Reduce heat level to med. Cook for 20-25 minutes, till tender when checked with fork.

Drain yuca. Remove fibers from middle, if any. Mash and cover yuca. Set it aside.

Heat oil on med-high in large-sized skillet.

Add bell peppers and onions. Cook till they soften, three minutes or so. Add scallion, garlic, cumin, kosher salt ground pepper. Stir often while cooking for about a minute.

Add ground beef. Cook till done fully through, usually six to seven minutes. Add tomato paste. Cook for two more minutes.

Remove skillet from heat. Adjust seasonings as desired. Allow to cool.

Divide yuca mixture in 10 balls. Poke holes through centers of all balls using a finger.

Place 1 tbsp. filling in each hole. Close balls gently. They should be oval shaped now.

Heat oil to 350F in large-sized pot. Add carimañolas you made in steps 7 8 to heated oil. Cook for two to three minutes, till they are golden brown in color. Turn them frequently.

Remove carimañolas from oil. Drain on layers of paper towels and serve them warm.

Panamanian Avocado Shrimp

If you have avocados that you need to use before they go bad, this is a perfect dish to make. The shrimp flavor, together with that of the avocados, Makes a wonderful lunch or dinner.

Makes 2 Servings

Cooking + Prep Time: 40 minutes

Ingredients:

- 1 avocado, large
- 1/2 pkg. of shrimp, frozen thawed
- 1 onion +/- as desired
- 3 sweet peppers, various colors +/- as desired
- 2 tbsp. of lemon juice, fresh
- 1/2 tsp. of seasoning, jerk
- 1/2 tsp. of pepper, ground
- 1 1/2 dash of seasoning, Cajun
- 1 tsp. of garlic, powdered
- 1 tbsp. of vinegar, white
- 3 tbsp. of oil, coconut

Instructions:

Add lemon juice, vinegar, ground pepper, jerk Cajun seasonings and garlic powder to shrimp. Mix till all the shrimp are seasoned evenly.

Add oil to heated pan. Sauté sweet peppers and onions.

Add the seasoned shrimp. Sauté till they become tender.

Slice the avocado into halves. Remove seed in center.

Pour the shrimp mixture into avocado indentations and serve.

Tamal de Olla

This dish is somewhat like what you would call Panama's answer to a shepherd's pie. It's made with chicken, olives and plenty of capers.

Makes 4-6 Servings

Cooking + Prep Time: 1 1/2 hour + 1 hour marinating time

Ingredients:

- 1 cup of wine, red
- 4 tbsp. of Worcestershire sauce, low sodium
- 5 garlic cloves
- 2 skinless, boneless chicken breasts
- 1/4 cup of oil, olive
- 1 diced onion, medium
- 1 tbsp. of Annatto seeds
- 5 diced Ajiés dulces sweet peppers
- 1 julienned pepper, red
- 1 julienned pepper, green
- 1/2 cup of pitted sliced olives, green
- 4 tbsp. of recaito cooking base
- 1 x 15-ounce can of tomato sauce, low sodium
- 1 cup of broth, chicken
- 1 pound of masa harina dried corn dough
- 3 1/2 ounces of capers

Instructions:

Combine 1/2 cup red wine, Worcestershire sauce 2 garlic cloves to make your marinade. Add chicken. Refrigerate it for an hour or longer to marinate.

Add oil and the annatto seeds to large pot. Heat over low while stirring for several minutes. Oil will start turning red in color. Remove and discard annatto seeds.

Raise pot heat up to high. Cut the chicken in smaller pieces. Fry in oil, being sure all sides are browned. Remove and reserve.

Slice onions, peppers, ajiés dulces olives.

Bring heat level to med-low. Add onions, peppers, recaito and remainder of garlic to pot. Cook till vegetables soften.

Add last 1/2 cup red wine, then chicken broth and tomato sauce. Return chicken to pot. Simmer for 12-15 minutes till chicken cooks through.

As chicken cooks, prepare masa. Add warm water to masa harina in large-sized bowl. Stir well. Masa should end up with a mashed potato-like consistency. It usually will require four to five cups of filtered water for this to happen.

After chicken cooks, remove pieces from the sauce. Shred them into a medium bowl.

Place chicken shreds back in sauce. Add capers and olives. Simmer as you prepare baking dish.

Preheat oven to 375F. To a 2-inch high baking dish, add thin masa layer to bottom. Press to all four sides evenly. Add filling to baking dish, without adding lots of liquid. Leave 1/2-inch without filling at the top.

Cover the baking dish with the aluminum foil and bake for 20-25 minutes. Remove foil. Bake for five to seven more minutes, till top masa layer starts browning. Serve hot.

Meat Potato Pie

Unlike empanadas, which are single-serving pies, this is more like a casserole. It tastes its best when made at home with the freshest ingredients.

Makes 4 Servings

Cooking + Prep Time: 50 minutes

Ingredients:

For the potato mixture

- 4 pounds of potatoes, white
- 4 ounces of cream cheese, low-fat

For the meat mixture

- 1/2 pound of beef, ground
- 3/4 cup of chopped ham, cooked, smoked
- 1/2 pkg. of small strip-cut bacon
- 1 green pepper, small
- 1/2 onion, medium
- 2 tbsp. of sofrito sauce, prepared
- 2 tbsp. of oil, olive
- 1 bunch of cilantro
- Salt, kosher, as desired
- Pepper, ground, as desired

For the toppings

- 1 medium egg, free range
- 1/2 cup of cheddar cheese shreds
- 1/2 cup of mozzarella cheese shreds

Instructions:

Preheat oven to 400F.

Chop onions, peppers and cilantro.

Place pan on stovetop burner. Add peppers, onions, bacon, ham, sofrito sauce, cilantro and oil. Fry till onion becomes glossy.

Add ground beef, kosher salt ground pepper to pan. Cook mixture fully.

Peel and cube-cut potatoes. Add kosher salt to water. Boil till potatoes are cooked tender. Mash them well. Add cream cheese + 2 tbsp. grease from cooked meat. Mix well.

Grease a pan lightly. Place 1/2 of potatoes on bottom, topped with a layer of meat mixture. Then follow with remainder of potato mixture. Beat egg pour on top. Add cheese shreds.

Bake in 400F oven till potatoes are golden on top. Allow to cool a bit before serving.

Panamanians have some wonderful dessert recipes. Here are a few...

Panamanian Sweet Milk Eggs

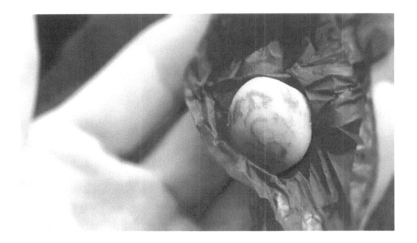

These sweet candies are easy to make, and you can make a larger batch if you'd like. They are wonderful for kid's parties, picnics, or afternoon teas with a friend.

Makes 2 Servings

Cooking + Prep Time: 35 minutes

Ingredients:

- 2 bottles dairy milk, whole
- 2 lbs. sugar, granulated
- 1 tsp. salt, kosher

Instructions:

Mix sugar kosher salt into milk. Pour into steel pot while constantly stirring.

Remove pot from the heat. Use mixture to form small sized balls. After they cool, wrap them in varied colors of paper. Serve or give as gifts.

Panamanian Coconut Cookies

These delectable cookies are somewhat similar to macaroons, but instead of being made with eggs, they are made using sweetened condensed milk. Everyone seems to love them!

Makes 4 Servings

Cooking + Prep Time: 35 minutes

Ingredients:

- 3 1/2 cups of sweetened coconut shreds
- 3/4 cup of sweetened milk, condensed
- 2 1/2 tbsp. of cornstarch
- 1 tsp. of vanilla extract, pure
- 1/2 tsp. of almond extract, pure

Instructions:

Preheat the oven to 375F.

Mix all ingredients together in medium bowl. Allow to set for five minutes or so.

Drop balls about 1 tbsp. in size on parchment paper-lined baking sheet. Allow an inch between them.

Bake for 12-15 minutes and watch them closely. Remove when they're light brown in color. Allow them to cool on wire rack. Serve plain or sprinkled with confectioner's sugar.

Mango Pudding

This pudding is natural to make for people who live in Panama, where mango trees are found in many areas. It may take a bit more work in colder climates to find mangoes, but it's worth the effort.

Makes 8 Servings

Cooking + Prep Time: 45 minutes

Ingredients:

- 4 cups of mangoes, sliced
- 1 1/2 cups of sugar, granulated
- 1/2 tsp. of cinnamon, ground
- 1/4 tsp. of allspice, ground
- 1 cup of flour, all-purpose
- 1 tsp. of baking soda, sodium-free
- 1/2 cup milk, whole
- 1/2 cup of butter, melted
- Ice cream, vanilla, as desired
- A pinch of salt, kosher

Instructions:

Mix mangoes with cinnamon, allspice and 1/2 of sugar in baking dish.

Mix remainder of sugar with milk, baking soda, flour, butter and kosher salt. Pour that mixture over mangoes.

Bake in 350F oven for 30-35 minutes. Remove and serve with vanilla ice cream, as desired.

Little Ears Cookies – Orejitas

These cookies look just like their names sound, like little ears. They're easy to make, too, with only four ingredients.

Makes 16 Servings

Cooking + Prep Time: 35 minutes

Ingredients:

- 1 x 8-ounce can of dinner rolls, refrigerated
- 1/4 cup of sugar, granulated
- 2 tbsp. of butter, melted
- Sugar, coarse, for sprinkling

Instructions:

Heat the oven to 375F. Line a baking sheet using parchment paper.

Separate rolls into four rectangles, each 7" x 4".

Sprinkle cutting board with 1 tbsp. sugar. Place two rectangles of dough on the sugar and lightly press. Brush the dough tops with 1 tbsp. of butter and sprinkle with a tbsp. of sugar.

Place rectangles on atop another. Roll short sides and make them meet in middle.

Repeat steps two through four.

Cut rolls into eight slices each. Place on the cookie sheet with two inches between them. Use coarse sugar to sprinkle. Press them slightly, flattening them a bit.

Bake cookies for 10-13 minutes, till golden brown in color. Cool for a minute and remove them from the cookie sheets. Allow to finish cooling and serve.

Raspado

These are tasty snow cones that children like to enjoy after school. Shaved ice is easy to make by whirling the ice cubes in your food processor.

Makes 4 Servings

Cooking + Prep Time: 35 minutes

Ingredients:

- 2 1/2 cups of chopped strawberries, fresh
- 3 tbsp. of sugar, granulated
- 6 cups of ice, shaved

Instructions:

Place two cups of strawberries in medium-sized pan with a cup of water 3 tbsp. sugar. Bring to boil and reduce the heat level to low.

Stir occasionally while cooking till sugar has dissolved and strawberries soften, two to three minutes. Remove them from heat. Allow to cool till not steaming anymore, eight to 10 minutes.

Pour the cooked strawberries plus syrup into food processor. Puree till you have a smooth texture. Allow to completely cool.

For each snow cone, fill 12-14-ounce glass or cup 1/2-way with the shaved ice. Pour 1/3 cup of strawberry syrup over the top. Fill the cup with additional shaved ice and 1/3 cup more of syrup. Top snow cones with 2 tbsp. of chopped strawberries. Serve.

Conclusion

This Panama cookbook has shown you…

… How to use different ingredients to affect unique Latin American tastes in dishes both well-known and rare.

How can you include Panamanian ingredients and techniques in your home recipes?

You can…

- Make Panamanian ceviche, which you may already know about. It is just as tasty as you may have heard.
- Learn to cook with masa harina, which is widely used in Panama. Find it in cooking or breakfast aisles in food markets.
- Enjoy making the delectable seafood dishes of Panama, including sea bass, shrimp and snapper. Fish is a mainstay in the region, and there are SO many ways to make it great.
- Make dishes using plantains and yuca, which are often used in Panama cooking.

- Make various types of desserts like ear-shaped cookies and sweet milk eggs that will tempt your family's sweet tooth.

Have fun experimenting! Enjoy the results!

Author's Afterthoughts

Thanks ever so much to each of my cherished readers for investing the time to read this book!

I know you could have picked from many other books, but you chose this one. So, a big thanks for reading all the way to the end. If you enjoyed this book or received value from it, I'd like to ask you for a favor. Please take a few minutes to **post an honest and heartfelt review on** Amazon.com. Your support does make a difference and helps to benefit other people.

Thanks!

Julia Chiles

About the Author

Julia Chiles

(1951-present)

Julia received her culinary degree from Le Counte' School of Culinary Delights in Paris, France. She enjoyed cooking more than any of her former positions. She lived in Montgomery, Alabama most of her life. She married Roger

Chiles and moved with him to Paris as he pursued his career in journalism. During the time she was there, she joined several cooking groups to learn the French cuisine, which inspired her to attend school and become a great chef.

Julia has achieved many awards in the field of food preparation. She has taught at several different culinary schools. She is in high demand on the talk show circulation, sharing her knowledge and recipes. Julia's favorite pastime is learning new ways to cook old dishes.

Julia is now writing cookbooks to add to her long list of achievements. The present one consists of favorite recipes as well as a few culinary delights from other cultures. She expands everyone's expectations on how to achieve wonderful dishes and not spend a lot of money. Julia firmly believes a wonderful dish can be prepare out of common household staples.

If anyone is interested in collecting Julia's cookbooks, check out your local bookstores and online. They are a big seller whatever venue you choose to purchase from.

Made in United States
Troutdale, OR
12/06/2024

25975455R00061